2

4

7

8

9

10

11

12

14

16

18

19

22

24

26

27

28

29

31

33

34

35

39

41

43

45

46

47

49

50

PUBLISHER'S WORDS

ABOUT PUBLIC DOMAIN AND POLITICAL CORRECTNESS

The concept of public domain is not understood by a lot of people. Today when a book is created – or music, or art, or just about anything – the right to copy and sell it belongs to the person who created it. If you write a book tomorrow, those rights would belong to you, even if you don't take the time, money and effort to register it with the copyright office. Eventually that right would expire, though for most of us, we'd be long gone. Generations ago the copyright laws were more complicated and restrictive. The rights holder had to file certain papers at certain times, and place a notice is very specific ways in the publication or the book would become public domain. Public domain means that *everyone* owns the rights to it. Anyone can reproduce a book in the public domain, and sell or distribute it however he/she sees fit. Anything published before 1923 in in the public domain, and about 85% of everything from 1924-1963 are, too. It's difficult to know for sure, and finding out if a specific work is in public domain can be time-consuming and expensive, but to save you the trouble UP History and Hobby reprints many titles in the public domain, legally and properly. So enjoy!*

Comics reflect their times. Many of the ideas expressed in comics of the 40's and 50's contain racism, ethnocentrism, bigotry, sexism, and a whole list of other -isms that today people would find offensive and unacceptable. Part of the reason we leave these as they were is because they are a picture of the times, in many ways a historical document. It is a time that will never come again, so we should preserve what it was, even with its scars and wrinkles.

Kari Therrian - Publisher

* UP History and Hobby also publishes many books which are NOT in the public domain. Only those which specifically state they are public domain are copyright-free. The rest have all rights reserved.